Expect to find out more about yourself and how to make your retirement a fulfilling adventure...... Excerpts:

"BORN FROM SEPTEMBER 18 TO OCTOBER 18:
Your cool logic, deep sense of responsibility and strong ethics bestow the perfect 'bridge over troubled water' to help heal, protect and maintain our fragile human dignity."

"BORN FROM OCTOBER 1955 TO OCTOBER 1956:
Depending on when you read this book, a great opportunity came about or will come about in the time period August 2015 to August 2016. What follows is a description of the nature of this opportunity: *Your ability to present yourself with great flair and finesse and capture the attention of an audience is extraordinary at this time of your life."*

"BORN FROM MARCH, 1958 TO FEBRUARY, 1961:
...challenges....... in the time period March, 2017 to January, 2020. What follows is a description of the circumstances that would have surfaced or will surface: *Your faith in your belief system is being tested to the fullest and there are cracks that are forming that you had never imagined would have appeared."*

Retirement Tables, providing information such as:

Monthly Cash Draw	$1,000	$2,000	$3,000
(Monthly Cash Draws will be annually increased by inflation)	Required Savings:	Required Savings:	Required Savings:
Using 100% Taxable Savings	$242,000	$484,000	$726,000
Using 100% Non-Tax. Savings	$206,000	$412,000	$617,000

This book is dedicated to my Mother, Zita

"You float, I float"
A pencil sketch
by Zita's granddaughter, Alexis

ACKNOWLEDGEMENTS

I would like to express my gratitude to all the wonderful musicians, singers, songwriters, actors, filmmakers and poets of my Generation for enriching our lives.

Author in 1970

TABLE OF CONTENTS

An Introduction

The music sessions normally begin an hour before lunch in the lounge of the care home that my Mom is now living in. She and the other folks who sing along to "Blue Moon" all have advancing Alzheimer's, but they sure can remember the words to this song. Music is one of the few memories that remain and bring smiles to their faces.

I wonder what songs we, the baby boomers, will be singing in our care home lounges when our turn arrives. Maybe we'll be yowling, "I can't get no satisfaction" or whispering, "the answer is blowing in the wind". Whatever the songs will be, I am sure we will remember the words and cherish their memory. They are deeply embedded in our cortex as this musical memory was developed in our early, impressionable years.

I wrote this book to help my generation *embrace* retirement. Guidance using *sidereal astrology* is provided   for your contemplation along with some serious-looking money charts for those that are worried about having enough money.

The songs that were included in this book, from a selection of a gazillion amazing songs of my generation released in our formative years, were chosen based on how they complemented the mood or meaning of the Zodiac archetypes that were described alongside.

If you believe that astrology is meaningful and helpful, I encourage you to obtain your sidereal astrological chart to know your true Sun and planetary signs. You can check out the website www.sidscopes.com for more information. I will refrain from knocking traditional 'tropical' astrology other than saying it uses incorrect planetary Zodiac placements from the perspective of astronomical science.

CHAPTER 1

MY GENERATION

"Why don't you all f-fade away
Talkin' 'bout my generation
Don't try to dig what we all s-s-s-
say
Talkin' 'bout my generation
I'm not trying to 'cause a big s-s-
sensation
Talkin' 'bout my generation
I'm just talkin' 'bout my g-g-g-
generation
Talkin' 'bout my generation"

Lyrics from the Song
"My Generation"
by *The Who*, 1965

The Song, "My Generation" is part of The Rock and Roll Hall of Fame's 500 Songs that 'Shaped Rock and Roll' and was inducted into the Grammy Hall of Fame for "historical, artistic and significant" value."

Source: Wikipedia

"My Generation" are those folks born from *1946 to 1964*, fondly known as the 'Baby Boomers'. It is the Boomers who can lay claim to the term, "generation", that by definition, "refers to a *group of people born and living during the same time*"

The boomers think of themselves as a *special* generation, and that is because, well, *they are*. After all, they witnessed man walking on the Moon, the civil-rights and the women's rights movements, anti-war and anti-establishment protests, drug delusions, sex on the Pill, raging inflation, the Beatles and James Brown on Ed Sullivan, Laugh-In's Ernestine, Mork's "Na-nu-na-nu", and the Fonz's thumbs-up "Eeey".

A record setting 73 million people tuned in to the Ed Sullivan Show on the evening of Feb. 9, 1964 making it a 'smashing' moment in television history. Do you remember where you were that night? Most boomers do.

The most enduring expression of my generation was music – Folk, Rock, Rhythm and Blues, Soul, Reggae, Country, Jazz - it was through music they identified themselves and expressed their values of freedom and social justice, their cynicism, their drug trips, their love for humanity, their yearning for mates, and their desire for peace. It was a *golden age* for music.

In America, the boomers encompass just over a quarter of the population, a relatively large chunk that amounts to around 76 million individuals.

ABBA

Marketers have followed this population bulge from this generation's childhood onwards. Capitalism and consumerism had flourished as businesses competed to satisfy the maturing boomers' wants - *like one-piece bell-bottom getups, hot pants and go-go boots.*

When I'm drivin' in my car
And that man comes on the radio
And he's tellin' me more and more
About some useless information
Supposed to drive my imagination
I can't get no, no no
Hey hey hey, that's what I say
I can't get no satisfaction

Lyrics from "No Satisfaction" by the Rolling Stones, 1965

The boomer generation is currently the richest consumer segment in the economy. Wealth management is a flourishing industry as advisors try to help boomers figure out how to finance their remaining years in the style they have envisioned. Statistics indicate that most boomers' retirement savings are short of the amounts needed.

The financial crisis of 2008 exposed just how volatile financial markets can be and how quickly the boomers' retirement nest eggs could be fried when markets turned ugly. This just added to their *fear* of retiring based on financial concerns.

In 2011, the oldest baby boomers turned 65. An AARP Study at this time showed that the vast majority of those turning 65 were optimistic, wanted to spend more time with their loved ones and make more time to do the things they always wanted to do. Most did not intend to move.

The boomers are setting a different tone for retirement as compared with their parents, just like they did for all the other earlier phases of their life. Unlike their parents, many of the boomers consider work to be part of retirement and many say they will never consider themselves to be retired. "Staying mentally and physically active" and "connected with others" outranked "money" as reasons to continue working.

This is wishful thinking often compromised by health and family issues. In reality, about *half* of the boomers turning 65 in the AARP Study were already retired, and around a third of those who were still employed said they had retired from a previous career. The odds are you are going to *have to* retire from your career.

Retirement is an *inevitable* happening in the life of most boomers - *face it* folks and embrace it!

"Living life is fun and we've just begun
To get our share of the world's delights
High hopes we have for the future
And our goal's in sight

No, we don't get depressed
Here's what we call our golden rule
Have faith in you and the things you do
You won't go wrong, this is our family jewel

We are family
I got all my sisters with me
We are family
Get up everybody and sing"

Lyrics from
"We Are Family"
by Sister Sledge, 1979

CHAPTER 2

RETIREMENT MONEY ISSUES

"You've got to know
when to hold 'em
Know when to fold 'em
Know when to walk away
And know when to run
You never count your money
When you're sittin' at the table
There'll be time enough
for countin'
When the dealin's done"

Lyrics from the song "The Gambler"
by Kenny Rogers, 1978

With retirement comes money, money, and money decisions that have to be reckoned with.

When should you start receiving your government pension, what are your company retirement plan options, how much and when should you withdraw your savings subject to tax and savings not subject to tax?

There are unknowns like your future health care costs and the market values of your assets. Family living circumstances could dramatically change.

Caveat emptor: It can make a positive difference in your lifestyle if there are two people generating income for living expenses. But the divorce rate among adults ages 50 and older has doubled since the 90's and roughly 1 in 4 divorces occur to persons ages 50 and older. Sadly, the rate of divorce was 2.5 times higher for those in remarriages versus first marriages.

"They say we're young and we don't know
We won't find out until we grow
Well I don't know if all that's true
'Cause you got me, and baby I got you
Babe
I got you babe I got you babe
They say our love won't pay the rent
Before it's earned, our money's all been spent
guess that's so, we don't have a pot
But at least I'm sure of all the things we got
Babe
I got you babe I got you babe"

Lyrics from "I've Got You Babe" by Sony and Cher, 1965

Some money answers are straight-forward and others have more shades of grey. One number you are forced to figure out pretty quickly when you retire and no longer have a steady paycheck is *what monthly dollar amount* is required to afford you a lifestyle that you deem essential for your well-being. And if your income sources and savings are low, then you will have to be very critical of those essentials in order to keep your head above water.

When doing the math for a retirement financial plan, you have to factor in how long you are going to live. We all know there is no way to predict for sure how long you are going to live. Stats say that in our culture women live to around 87 years of age nowadays and men to 85 years, but we all know those numbers are simply just average numbers.

How you spread your savings out over your remaining years is a *continuous* balancing act. You are more apt to spend more in your early retirement years on interests like travelling and hobbies, and you are more likely to spend a greater proportion of your income on health care in your latter years.

MONTHLY EXPENSES

There is no way around doing any money projections unless you know what you bucks you need to stay afloat. You can figure this out by simply adding up all of your monthly expenses. If you use a credit card to pay for your purchases, you can refer to some 'normal' monthly statements to see what your burn amount is. Then include your costs for taxes, rent/mortgage, insurance and other inescapable money-eating burdens. Divide annual expenses by 12 to keep everything as a monthly tally. The final total will indicate what amount of cash you figure you need to live on every month for the year. Your life's circumstances may change; then you will have to revise your numbers.

REQUIRED MONTHLY CASH DRAWS

Now that you know what your current monthly expenses are, you will have to determine what amount of monthly income you are receiving on a regular basis. This includes your primary sources of steady income provided by government senior pension plans, and other contracted sources such as annuity payments from a pension plan by your former employer or property rental income.

Then you can determine your monthly *cash shortfall* (if any) after you subtract your income from your expenses. That shortfall will have to be made up with your savings as it is unlikely lenders will continue to supply you with money if you don't have steady employment income (and you don't want to leave your kids with your debt). If the balance is negative and there is no shortfall, you can party hearty and your kids *may* get an inheritance.

My Monthly Expenses   ?

—

My Monthly Income   ?

_____

Monthly Shortfall (Surplus)   ?

Formula for Making-Ends-Meet:
Expenses - Income = 0   or   Expenses = Income

AFTER-TAX MONTHLY DRAWS FROM SAVINGS

What follows are Tables that are designed to show you the *dollar amount of savings* that are required in order to provide an *after-tax monthly cash draw* that ranges from a $1,000 per month withdrawal to a $3,000 per month withdrawal *in today's dollars.* You can select the Table that indicates this income flow for the next 10 years, 15 years, 20 years or 25 years. If you need more fine tuning, you can just *divide or multiply* whatever amounts you need *to adjust for cash flow* and do the same math with the associated dollar amount of required savings shown in the Table. Do not add or subtract as the math won't hold.

Your savings can be in two forms depending on the taxation treatment of withdrawals. The first nest egg is that of *'taxable savings'*, such as retirement savings accounts where withdrawals are 100% taxable and you must include them as taxable income when you file your tax returns.

Taxable savings withdrawals are taxed at the *'marginal tax rate'* and the Tables provide two, namely 15% and 25% marginal tax rates. The rate you use depends on your income level and your corresponding tax bracket which you can readily find using 'tax calculators' offered on the internet. If you are in a higher marginal tax rate than 25%, chances are you don't have to worry about retirement income.

The other nest-egg is in the form of *'non-taxable savings'*, like investment accounts that pay dividends and interest, where the 'capital' you withdraw is tax-free, aside from capital-gains tax. Government-regulated tax free savings accounts are also included as 'non-taxable savings'.

Many boomers have both kinds of savings accounts, and so the Tables provide not only 100% of savings in either taxable savings or non-taxable savings' stashes, but also a mix of the two nest eggs where 50% of withdrawals are required from each one, as well as scenarios of 75%/25% and 25%/75% of withdrawals from the two respective nest eggs.

ASSET ALLOCATION MIX OF INVESTMENTS IN SAVINGS

Another important variable is embedded in the Tables. That is your *overall investment portfolio's 'asset allocation mix'*. Ask your financial advisor or a friend in-the-know if you don't know what it is. The Table math requires the combined mix of all the investments in both your taxable savings' accounts and non-taxable savings' accounts'. It is likely that you may have completely different mixes in these accounts so it can take a bit of figuring out what the overall mix is. This may lead to a very informative discussion with your financial advisor. There are two scenarios for you to choose from in the Tables, namely 60% Equity (stocks) and 40% Fixed Income (bonds) or the reverse, 40% Equity and 60% Fixed Income. Choose the one that your overall investment mix comes closest to. Use the 40% Equity/ 60% Fixed Income Tables if you don't know.

If you have more equity than 60%, you will be subject to more risk (volatility - ouch, 2008!) but arguably, have the potential for higher returns. If you do have more, it is time to get proper investment advice.

ASSUMED RATES OF INVESTMENT RETURNS

A 6% annual rate of return is assumed for Equity and a 4% annual rate of return is assumed for Fixed Income, after or net of *management fees; (fees should be at most 1%, or preferably lower)*. That yields an annual nominal rate of return for a *60% Equity/ 40% Fixed Income* portfolio of **5.2%** and **4.8%** for a *40% Equity/ 60% Fixed Income* portfolio. I would not expect the average actual return over the rest of our lives to be significantly higher. I believe we are entering a period that will probably last until the end of the lives of the boomers, where the returns from equity markets will be dampened by the effects of the baby boomer's slowing consumption of goods and services and inflation will remain low.

ASSUMED RATE OF INFLATION

Inflation is set at **2%** in the Tables, a rate the Fed would *like* to maintain. Inflation is important to recognize. The Tables indicate *after-tax monthly cash flows in today's dollars.* That means that you can expect to reap from your required savings, inflated draws for each subsequent year. For example, the math takes into account

$2,000 a month after year one will change to a required $2,040 a month come year two, $2,080 a month come year three, and so on, and the dollar amounts shown for your required savings take this inflation into account. If all the scenario variables hold true and the averages are actually realized, you can more of less be assured of keeping up with inflation. *Just find out if your income sources are indexed for inflation.*

FAR OUT! RETIREMENT SAVINGS TABLES

These Tables are meant to help you keep track of your savings and what your nest eggs can afford you. You can get an approximate picture right away of what amount of monthly cash you can get your hands on, depending on your 'Scenario'. For example, have a look at Scenario A. If you currently have savings of around $350,000 in your taxable retirement savings account and around $100,000 in your non-taxable investment account and you want to fund retirement for 25 years with a 60% Equity/ 40% Fixed Income overall investment mix, then you are looking at having an after-tax cash draw of around $2,000 a month cash to spend. "Mercy, Mercy, Me" (*Marvin Gaye, 1971*).

Scenario A
*(as in "**A**in't No Sunshine" by Bill Withers, 1971)*

Time period for payout: **25** years to fund
Investment Mix: **60%** Equities / **40%** Fixed Income
Expected Average Rate of Inflation: 2%
Expected Average Rate of Return on Equities: 6%
Expected Average Rate of Return on Bonds: 4%
Marginal Tax Rate: **15%**

Annual Cash Draw	$12,000	$24,000	$36,000
Monthly Cash Draw	**$1,000**	**$2,000**	**$3,000**
(Monthly Cash Draws will be	Required	Required	Required
annually increased by inflation)	Savings:	Savings:	Savings:
Using 100% Taxable Savings	$242,000	$484,000	$726,000
Using 100% Non-Tax. Savings	$206,000	$412,000	$617,000
Using 75% Taxable Savings +	$182,000	$363,000	$545,000
25% Non-Taxable Savings	$52,000	$103,000	$154,000
Using 50% Taxable Savings +	$121,000	$242,000	$363,000
50% Non-Taxable Savings	$103,000	$206,000	$309,000
Using 25% Taxable Savings +	$61,000	$121,000	$182,000
75% Non-Taxable Savings	$154,000	$309,000	$463,000

All data provided by Avenex Financial Corp., BC, Canada

SCENARIO B

(as in "Black Magic Woman" by Santana, 1970)

Time period for payout: **20** years to fund
Investment Mix: **60%** Equities / **40%** Fixed Income
Expected Average Rate of Inflation: 2%
Expected Average Rate of Return on Equities: 6%
Expected Average Rate of Return on Bonds: 4%
Marginal Tax Rate: **15%**

Annual Cash Draw	$12,000	$24,000	$36,000
Monthly Cash Draw	**$1,000**	**$2,000**	**$3,000**
(Monthly Cash Draws will be	Required	Required	Required
annually increased by inflation)	Savings:	Savings:	Savings:
Using 100% Taxable Savings	$207,000	$415,000	$622,000
Using 100% Non-Tax. Savings	$176,000	$353,000	$528,000
Using 75% Taxable Savings +	$156,000	$311,000	$467,000
25% Non-Taxable Savings	$44,000	$88,000	$132,000
Using 50% Taxable Savings +	$104,000	$207,000	$311,000
50% Non-Taxable Savings	$88,000	$176,000	$264,000
Using 25% Taxable Savings +	$52,000	$104,000	$156,000
75% Non-Taxable Savings	$132,000	$264,000	$397,000

All data provided by Avenex Financial Corp., BC, Canada

SCENARIO C
(as in "Can't Get Enough of Your Love" by Barry White, 1974)

Time period for payout: **15** years to fund
Investment Mix: **60%** Equities / **40%** Fixed Income
Expected Average Rate of Inflation: 2%
Expected Average Rate of Return on Equities: 6%
Expected Average Rate of Return on Bonds: 4%
Marginal Tax Rate: **15%**

Annual Cash Draw	$12,000	$24,000	$36,000
Monthly Cash Draw	**$1,000**	**$2,000**	**$3,000**
(Monthly Cash Draws will be	Required	Required	Required
annually increased by inflation)	Savings:	Savings:	Savings:
Using 100% Taxable Savings	$167,000	$334,000	$501,000
Using 100% Non-Tax. Savings	$142,000	$284,000	$426,000
Using 75% Taxable Savings +	$125,000	$250,000	$375,000
25% Non-Taxable Savings	$35,000	$71,000	$106,000
Using 50% Taxable Savings +	$83,000	$167,000	$250,000
50% Non-Taxable Savings	$71,000	$142,000	$213,000
Using 25% Taxable Savings +	$42,000	$83,000	$125,000
75% Non-Taxable Savings	$106,000	$213,000	$319,000

All data provided by Avenex Financial Corp., BC, Canada

Scenario D
(as in "Daniel" by Elton John, 1973)

Time period for payout: **10** years to fund
Investment Mix: **60%** Equities / **40%** Fixed Income
Expected Average Rate of Inflation: 2%
Expected Average Rate of Return on Equities: 6%
Expected Average Rate of Return on Bonds: 4%
Marginal Tax Rate: **15%**

Annual Cash Draw	$12,000	$24,000	$36,000
Monthly Cash Draw	**$1,000**	**$2,000**	**$3,000**
(Monthly Cash Draws will be annually increased by inflation)	Required Savings:	Required Savings:	Required Savings:
Using 100% Taxable Savings	$120,000	$240,000	$360,000
Using 100% Non-Tax. Savings	$102,000	$203,000	$305,000
Using 75% Taxable Savings + 25% Non-Taxable Savings	$90,000 $25,000	$179,000 $51,000	$269,000 $76,000
Using 50% Taxable Savings + 50% Non-Taxable Savings	$60,000 $51,000	$119,000 $102,000	$179,000 $152,000
Using 25% Taxable Savings + 75% Non-Taxable Savings	$30,000 $76,000	$60,000 $152,000	$90,000 $229,000

All data provided by Avenex Financial Corp., BC, Canada

SCENARIO E
(as in "Every Time You Go Away", Paul Young, 1985)

Time period for payout: **25** years to fund
Investment Mix: **40%** Equities / **60%** Fixed Income
Expected Average Rate of Inflation: 2%
Expected Average Rate of Return on Equities: 6%
Expected Average Rate of Return on Bonds: 4%
Marginal Tax Rate: **15%**

Annual Cash Draw	$12,000	$24,000	$36,000
Monthly Cash Draw	**$1,000**	**$2,000**	**$3,000**
(Monthly Cash Draws will be	Required	Required	Required
annually increased by inflation)	Savings:	Savings:	Savings:
Using 100% Taxable Savings	$253,000	$506,000	$759,000
Using 100% Non-Tax. Savings	$215,000	$430,000	$645,000
Using 75% Taxable Savings +	$190,000	$379,000	$569,000
25% Non-Taxable Savings	$54,000	$108,000	$161,000
Using 50% Taxable Savings +	$126,000	$253,000	$379,000
50% Non-Taxable Savings	$108,000	$215,000	$323,000
Using 25% Taxable Savings +	$63,000	$126,000	$190,000
75% Non-Taxable Savings	$161,000	$323,000	$484,000

All data provided by Avenex Financial Corp., BC, Canada

Scenario F
(as in "Fame" by David Bowie, 1975)

Time period for payout: **20** years to fund
Investment Mix: **40%** Equities / **60%** Fixed Income
Expected Average Rate of Inflation: 2%
Expected Average Rate of Return on Equities: 6%
Expected Average Rate of Return on Bonds: 4%
Marginal Tax Rate: **15%**

Annual Cash Draw	$12,000	$24,000	$36,000
Monthly Cash Draw	**$1,000**	**$2,000**	**$3,000**
(Monthly Cash Draws will be	Required	Required	Required
annually increased by inflation)	Savings:	Savings:	Savings:
Using 100% Taxable Savings	$215,000	$430,000	$645,000
Using 100% Non-Tax. Savings	$183,000	$366,000	$548,000
Using 75% Taxable Savings +	$161,000	$323,000	$484,000
25% Non-Taxable Savings	$46.000	$91,000	$137,000
Using 50% Taxable Savings +	$108,000	$215,000	$323,000
50% Non-Taxable Savings	$91,000	$183,000	$274,000
Using 25% Taxable Savings +	$54,000	$108,000	$161,000
75% Non-Taxable Savings	$137,000	$274,000	$411,000

All data provided by Avenex Financial Corp., BC, Canada

Scenario G

*(as in "We **G**otta **G**et Out of this Place by Eric Burdon and the Animals, 1964)*

Time period for payout: **15** years to fund
Investment Mix: **40%** Equities / **60%** Fixed Income
Expected Average Rate of Inflation: 2%
Expected Average Rate of Return on Equities: 6%
Expected Average Rate of Return on Bonds: 4%
Marginal Tax Rate: **15%**

Annual Cash Draw	$12,000	$24,000	$36,000
Monthly Cash Draw	**$1,000**	**$2,000**	**$3,000**
(Monthly Cash Draws will be	Required	Required	Required
annually increased by inflation)	Savings:	Savings:	Savings:
Using 100% Taxable Savings	$172,000	$343,000	$515,000
Using 100% Non-Tax. Savings	$146,000	$292,000	$438,000
Using 75% Taxable Savings +	$129,000	$258,000	$386,000
25% Non-Taxable Savings	$36,000	$73,000	$109,000
Using 50% Taxable Savings +	$86,000	$172,000	$258,000
50% Non-Taxable Savings	$73,000	$146,000	$219,000
Using 25% Taxable Savings +	$43,000	$86,000	$129,000
75% Non-Taxable Savings	$109,000	$219,000	$328,000

All data provided by Avenex Financial Corp., BC, Canada

SCENARIO H
*(as in "**He**art of Gold" by Neil Young, 1972)*

Time period for payout: **10** years to fund
Investment Mix: **40%** Equities / **60%** Fixed Income
Expected Average Rate of Inflation: 2%
Expected Average Rate of Return on Equities: 6%
Expected Average Rate of Return on Bonds: 4%
Marginal Tax Rate: **15%**

Annual Cash Draw	$12,000	$24,000	$36,000
Monthly Cash Draw	**$1,000**	**$2,000**	**$3,000**
(Monthly Cash Draws will be	Required	Required	Required
annually increased by inflation)	Savings:	Savings:	Savings:
Using 100% Taxable Savings	$122,000	$244,000	$366,000
Using 100% Non-Tax. Savings	$104,000	$207,000	$311,000
Using 75% Taxable Savings +	$92,000	$183,000	$275,000
25% Non-Taxable Savings	$26,000	$52,000	$78,000
Using 50% Taxable Savings +	$61,000	$122,000	$183,000
50% Non-Taxable Savings	$52,000	$104,000	$156,000
Using 25% Taxable Savings +	$31,000	$61,000	$92,000
75% Non-Taxable Savings	$78,000	$156,000	$233,000

All data provided by Avenex Financial Corp., BC, Canada

SCENARIO I

(as in "I've Been Loving You Too Long" by Otis Redding, 1965)

Time period for payout: **25** years to fund
Investment Mix: **60%** Equities / **40%** Fixed Income
Expected Average Rate of Inflation: 2%
Expected Average Rate of Return on Equities: 6%
Expected Average Rate of Return on Bonds: 4%
Marginal Tax Rate: **25%**

Annual Cash Draw	$12,000	$24,000	$36,000
Monthly Cash Draw	**$1,000**	**$2,000**	**$3,000**
(Monthly Cash Draws will be	Required	Required	Required
annually increased by inflation)	Savings:	Savings:	Savings:
Using 100% Taxable Savings	$274,000	$548,000	$823,000
Using 100% Non-Tax. Savings	$208,000	$412,000	$617,000
Using 75% Taxable Savings +	$208,000	$416,000	$617,000
25% Non-Taxable Savings	$51,000	$103,000	$154,000
Using 50% Taxable Savings +	$137,000	$274,000	$416,000
50% Non-Taxable Savings	$103,000	$206,000	$309,000
Using 25% Taxable Savings +	$69,000	$137,000	$208,000
75% Non-Taxable Savings	$154,000	$309,000	$463,000

All data provided by Avenex Financial Corp., BC, Canada

SCENARIO J
(as in "Jive Talkin'" by the Bee Gees, 1975)

Time period for payout: **20** years to fund
Investment Mix: **60%** Equities / **40%** Fixed Income
Expected Average Rate of Inflation: 2%
Expected Average Rate of Return on Equities: 6%
Expected Average Rate of Return on Bonds: 4%
Marginal Tax Rate: **25%**

Annual Cash Draw	$12,000	$24,000	$36,000
Monthly Cash Draw	**$1,000**	**$2,000**	**$3,000**
(Monthly Cash Draws will be	Required	Required	Required
annually increased by inflation)	Savings:	Savings:	Savings:
Using 100% Taxable Savings	$235,000	$470,000	$705,000
Using 100% Non-Tax. Savings	$176,000	$353,000	$529,000
Using 75% Taxable Savings +	$176,000	$353,000	$529,000
25% Non-Taxable Savings	$44,000	$88,000	$132,000
Using 50% Taxable Savings +	$118,000	$235,000	$353,000
50% Non-Taxable Savings	$88,000	$176,000	$264,000
Using 25% Taxable Savings +	$59,000	$118,000	$176,000
75% Non-Taxable Savings	$132,000	$264,000	$397,000

All data provided by Avenex Financial Corp., BC, Canada

Scenario K

(as in "Kiss and Say Goodbye" by the Manhattans, 1976)

Time period for payout: **15** years to fund
Investment Mix: **60%** Equities / **40%** Fixed Income
Expected Average Rate of Inflation: 2%
Expected Average Rate of Return on Equities: 6%
Expected Average Rate of Return on Bonds: 4%
Marginal Tax Rate: 25%

Annual Cash Draw	$12,000	$24,000	$36,000
Monthly Cash Draw	**$1,000**	**$2,000**	**$3,000**
(Monthly Cash Draws will be	Required	Required	Required
annually increased by inflation)	Savings:	Savings:	Savings:
Using 100% Taxable Savings	$189,000	$378,000	$567,000
Using 100% Non-Tax. Savings	$142,000	$284,000	$426,000
Using 75% Taxable Savings +	$142,000	$284,000	$426,000
25% Non-Taxable Savings	$35,000	$71,000	$106,000
Using 50% Taxable Savings +	$95,000	$189,000	$284,000
50% Non-Taxable Savings	$71,000	$142,000	$213,000
Using 25% Taxable Savings +	$47,000	$95,000	$142,000
75% Non-Taxable Savings	$106,000	$213,000	$319,000

All data provided by Avenex Financial Corp., BC, Canada

SCENARIO L

(as in "Lady Love Me (One More Time)" by George Benson, 1983)

Time period for payout: **10** years to fund
Investment Mix: **60%** Equities / **40%** Fixed Income
Expected Average Rate of Inflation: 2%
Expected Average Rate of Return on Equities: 6%
Expected Average Rate of Return on Bonds: 4%
Marginal Tax Rate: **25%**

Annual Cash Draw	$12,000	$24,000	$36,000
Monthly Cash Draw	**$1,000**	**$2,000**	**$3,000**
(Monthly Cash Draws will be	Required	Required	Required
annually increased by inflation)	Savings:	Savings:	Savings:
Using 100% Taxable Savings	$136,000	$271,000	$407,000
Using 100% Non-Tax. Savings	$102,000	$203,000	$305,000
Using 75% Taxable Savings +	$102,000	$203,000	$305,000
25% Non-Taxable Savings	$25,000	$51,000	$76,000
Using 50% Taxable Savings +	$68,000	$136,000	$203,000
50% Non-Taxable Savings	$51,000	$102,000	$152,000
Using 25% Taxable Savings +	$34,000	$68,000	$102,000
75% Non-Taxable Savings	$76,000	$152,000	$229,000

All data provided by Avenex Financial Corp., BC, Canada

Scenario M
*(as in "**M**argaritaville" by Jimmy Buffet, 1976)*

Time period for payout: **25** years to fund
Investment Mix: **40%** Equities / **60%** Fixed Income
Expected Average Rate of Inflation: 2%
Expected Average Rate of Return on Equities: 6%
Expected Average Rate of Return on Bonds: 4%
Marginal Tax Rate: **25%**

Annual Cash Draw	$12,000	$24,000	$36,000
Monthly Cash Draw	**$1,000**	**$2,000**	**$3,000**
(Monthly Cash Draws will be	Required	Required	Required
annually increased by inflation)	Savings:	Savings:	Savings:
Using 100% Taxable Savings	$287,000	$573,000	$860,000
Using 100% Non-Tax. Savings	$215,000	$430,000	$645,000
Using 75% Taxable Savings +	$215,000	$430,000	$645,000
25% Non-Taxable Savings	$54,000	$108,000	$161,000
Using 50% Taxable Savings +	$143,000	$287,000	$430,000
50% Non-Taxable Savings	$108,000	$215,000	$323,000
Using 25% Taxable Savings +	$72,000	$143,000	$215,000
75% Non-Taxable Savings	$161,000	$323,000	$484,000

All data provided by Avenex Financial Corp., BC, Canada

SCENARIO N
(as in "Night Moves" by Bob Seger, 1976)

Time period for payout: **20** years to fund
Investment Mix: **40%** Equities / **60%** Fixed Income
Expected Average Rate of Inflation: 2%
Expected Average Rate of Return on Equities: 6%
Expected Average Rate of Return on Bonds: 4%
Marginal Tax Rate: **25%**

Annual Cash Draw	$12,000	$24,000	$36,000
Monthly Cash Draw	**$1,000**	**$2,000**	**$3,000**
(Monthly Cash Draws will be	Required	Required	Required
annually increased by inflation)	Savings:	Savings:	Savings:
Using 100% Taxable Savings	$244,000	$487,000	$731,000
Using 100% Non-Tax. Savings	$183,000	$366,000	$548,000
Using 75% Taxable Savings +	$183,000	$366,000	$548,000
25% Non-Taxable Savings	$46,000	$91,000	$137,000
Using 50% Taxable Savings +	$122,000	$244,000	$366,000
50% Non-Taxable Savings	$91,000	$183,000	$274,000
Using 25% Taxable Savings +	$61,000	$122,000	$183,000
75% Non-Taxable Savings	$137,000	$274,000	$411,000

All data provided by Avenex Financial Corp., BC, Canada

Scenario O
(as in "O-o-h Child" by the Five Stairsteps, 1970)

Time period for payout: **15** years to fund
Investment Mix: **40%** Equities / **60%** Fixed Income
Expected Average Rate of Inflation: 2%
Expected Average Rate of Return on Equities: 6%
Expected Average Rate of Return on Bonds: 4%
Marginal Tax Rate: **25%**

Annual Cash Draw	$12,000	$24,000	$36,000
Monthly Cash Draw	**$1,000**	**$2,000**	**$3,000**
(Monthly Cash Draws will be	Required	Required	Required
annually increased by inflation)	Savings:	Savings:	Savings:
Using 100% Taxable Savings	$195,000	$389,000	$584,000
Using 100% Non-Tax. Savings	$146,000	$292,000	$438,000
Using 75% Taxable Savings +	$146,000	$292,000	$438,000
25% Non-Taxable Savings	$36,000	$73,000	$109,000
Using 50% Taxable Savings +	$97,000	$195,000	$292,000
50% Non-Taxable Savings	$73,000	$146,000	$219,000
Using 25% Taxable Savings +	$49,000	$97,000	$146,000
75% Non-Taxable Savings	$109,000	$219,000	$328,000

All data provided by Avenex Financial Corp., BC, Canada

Scenario P
(as in "Peace Train" by Cat Stevens, 1971)

Time period for payout: **10** years to fund
Investment Mix: **40%** Equities / **60%** Fixed Income
Expected Average Rate of Inflation: 2%
Expected Average Rate of Return on Equities: 6%
Expected Average Rate of Return on Bonds: 4%
Marginal Tax Rate: **25%**

Annual Cash Draw	$12,000	$24,000	$36,000
Monthly Cash Draw	**$1,000**	**$2,000**	**$3,000**
(Monthly Cash Draws will be	Required	Required	Required
annually increased by inflation)	Savings:	Savings:	Savings:
Using 100% Taxable Savings	$138,000	$277,000	$415,000
Using 100% Non-Tax. Savings	$104,000	$207,000	$311,000
Using 75% Taxable Savings +	$104,000	$207,000	$311,000
25% Non-Taxable Savings	$26,000	$52,000	$78,000
Using 50% Taxable Savings +	$69,000	$138,000	$207,000
50% Non-Taxable Savings	$52,000	$104,000	$156,000
Using 25% Taxable Savings +	$35,000	$69,000	$104,000
75% Non-Taxable Savings	$78,000	$156,000	$233,000

All data provided by Avenex Financial Corp., BC, Canada

"You say you don't want no diamond rings
And I'll be satisfied
Tell me, if you want these kind of things
That money just can't buy
I may not have a lot to give
But what I got I'll give to you
I said, I don't care too much for money
'Cause money can't buy me love
Buy me love
Money can't buy me love"

Lyrics from the song
"Money Can't Buy Me Love"
by the Beatles, 1964

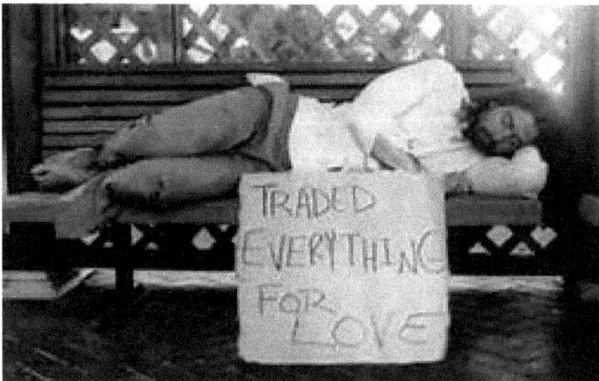

"When the moon is in the Seventh House
And Jupiter aligns with Mars
Then peace will guide the planets
And love will steer the stars

This is the dawning of the Age of Aquarius
The Age of Aquarius
Aquarius! Aquarius!

Harmony and understanding
Sympathy and trust abounding
No more falsehoods or derisions
Golden living dreams of visions
Mystic crystal revelation
And the mind's true liberation
Aquarius! Aquarius! "

Lyrics from the "Age of Aquarius",
a song from the 1967 musical "Hair"
released as a single by The Fifth Dimension, 1969

CHAPTER 3

THE SATURN RETIREMENT *ALARM* CLOCK

Starting at your time of birth, Saturn will take around 30 years to complete an orbit around the Sun and find itself back again in the same celestial position. When this happens, it is said that Saturn transits your 'natal Saturn' position. It is around this time that major challenges present themselves in your life.

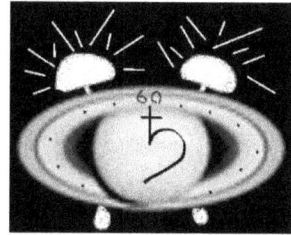

These challenges shake you to your roots and force you to face up to the realities of the present. You question your ways and wonder if you are living up to your potential. An inner force provides you with the courage to be able to leave behind the relics of your past and start deliberately putting in place what is necessary for an enhanced future that is yours to claim.

"*This was definitely a song with a purpose. I wanted to write a big song, some kind of theme song, with short concise verses that piled up on each other in a hypnotic way. The civil rights movement and the folk music movement were pretty close and allied together at that time.*"

Quote from Bob Dylan about this song
Source: Wikipedia

"*Come gather 'round people*
Wherever you roam
And admit that the waters
Around you have grown
And accept it that soon
You'll be drenched to the bone.
If your time to you
Is worth savin'
Then you better start swimmin'
Or you'll sink like a stone
For the times they are a-changin'."

Lyrics from the Song "Times They Are a-Changing" by Bob Dylan, 1964

As a baby-boomer, Saturn has already made this transit once in your life around the age of 30. The stretch of time when this occurred in your life is indicated in the description that follows. It is most probable that after this phase had passed, you found your life taking a totally different course. Thanks to the life lessons you experienced during the first Saturn transit, a maturity developed within you that would prove to serve you well for the rest of your life and fortify you for the next Saturn go-around.

The second time that this transit had occurred or will occur was, or is, around the age of 60. Based on the time you were born, you can read in the descriptions what the nature of Saturn's challenges had been or will entail. *If ever there was a time to retire, this transit would have delivered or will deliver the motivators.*

For those of you who have *already had experienced Saturn's second transit*, it is advisable that you reflect on Saturn's important lessons in order to understand how the Zodiac prepares you for your *ultimate mission* in life.

Jimi Hendrix is widely regarded as one of the most influential electric guitarists in the history of rock music. He died at the age of 27 in 1970. Source: Wikipedia

"Will the wind ever remember
The names it has blown in the past
And with his crutch, its old age, and its wisdom
It whispers no, this will be the last
And the wind cries Mary"

Lyrics from "The Wind Cries Mary"
by Jimi Hendrix, 1967

BORN FROM JANUARY 1946 TO JUNE, 1946

Reflect on the time period *July, 1973 to July, 1975*, as well as *May, 2003 to September, 2004*. What major changes came about in your life during those times when Saturn was at work? Were the circumstances occurring at those times similar to the description below?

Information sources that were normally readily accessible, are being subject to limitations. Lines of communications have additional barriers to deal with, such as more rules and regulations. This is making your need for instant feedback and up-to-date data difficult to satisfactorily achieve. Frustration is growing and given you are unable to change the system in place, you are faced with making major personal changes. If you don't, your mental health may suffer.

BORN FROM JULY, 1946 TO AUGUST, 1948

Reflect on the time period *August, 1975 to September, 1977,* as well as *October, 2004 to July, 2007.* What major changes came about in your life during those times when Saturn was at work? Were the circumstances occurring at those times similar to the description below?

You find yourself absorbed with trying to make sense of your emotions. What is coming to consciousness is how people whom you have had close relationships with are triggering feelings of anxiety. You find yourself questioning how your emotions are taking control of your thoughts and it is difficult for you to accomplish tasks. You no longer want to be subject to the roller coaster of your sentiments and desire emotional stability. It is time to face up to how you are reacting deep inside, accept these feelings for what they are, and do something concrete about them. This may involve taking tougher stances in life and facing up to realities.

Born from September, 1948 to October, 1950

Reflect on the time period *October, 1977 to November, 1979*, as well as *August, 2007 to September, 2009.* What major changes came about in your life during those times when Saturn was at work? Were the circumstances occurring at those times similar to the description below?

You are sensing that the effects of your actions are not being recognized and appreciated like they used to be. Your power of influence seems to be weakening and creative inspirations are waning. You are not one to be in a thankless, infertile environment and feel an urge to redirect your energy into other creative endeavors that you will be acknowledged for and bring back your zest for life. You recognize that you should let go of any childish practices that you have been hanging onto and move courageously forward with mature aspirations.

BORN FROM NOVEMBER, 1950 TO DECEMBER, 1952

Reflect on the time period *December, 1979 to October, 1982,* as well as *October, 2009 to November, 2011.* What major changes came about in your life during those times when Saturn was at work? Were the circumstances occurring at those times similar to the description below?

You cannot avoid addressing even the smallest of details. It seems that once you believe a project you have been working on is completed another loose end appears and you are drawn back into it. Day-to-day appeals for your attention are becoming personally uninviting and duties that were once simply doable are becoming laborious tasks. All of this may be affecting your health. You know you have to finish what you have started, but you also sense that a time is nearing where you just do not want to continue to make more commitments in your current environment.

"You just call out my name
And you know wherever I am
I'll come running, to see you again
Winter, spring, summer or fall
All you have to do is call
And I'll be there
You've got a friend"

Lyrics from "You've Got a Friend" by Carole King, 1971

Carole King had made 25 solo albums, and "Tapestry" held the record for the most weeks at Number 1 by a female artist for more than 20 years.

Source: Wikipedia

BORN FROM JANUARY 1953 TO NOVEMBER, 1955

Reflect on the time period *November, 1982 to December, 1984,* as well as *December, 2011 to November, 2014.* What major changes came about in your life during those times when Saturn was at work? Were the circumstances occurring at those times similar to the description below?

It is becoming more difficult to maintain harmony in some relationships. You sense you are being unduly pressured to conform and this is going against your personal ethics. This is emotionally draining and just can't go on. Compromises seem out of reach even though you are making diplomatic efforts to create an accord. The only solution may be to keep ground and stand up for what you believe in, then move on. Severing ties is never easy but this schism may be essential in order for you to progress in life.

BORN FROM DECEMBER, 1955 TO FEBRUARY, 1958

Reflect on the time period *January, 1985 to December, 1987*. What major change came about in your life at that time? Depending on when you read this book, the initiators of that change would have been or will be similar to those in the time period *December, 2014 to February, 2017*. What follows is a description of the circumstances that would have surfaced or will surface.

People that you thought to be trustworthy turn out not to be. Situations are just not turning out the way you expected them to as a result of secret motives of others. Your level of anxiety is increasing and your anger is rising. Change is going to have to be a consequence of bringing the facts into the open. Do not doubt your intuition and keep in mind your level of trusting others is at an all- time low. You will be a much better reader of people as a consequence of uncovering this deception.

BORN FROM MARCH, 1958 TO FEBRUARY, 1961

Reflect on the time period *January, 1988 to April, 1990*. What major change came about in your life at that time? Depending on when you read this book, the initiators of that change would have been or will be similar to those in the time period *March, 2017 to January, 2020*. What follows is a description of the circumstances that would have surfaced or will surface.

Your faith in your belief system is being tested to the fullest and there are cracks that are forming that you had never imagined would have appeared. You are questioning why you do what you do and its true value to humanity. What was once exciting and promised great opportunity now seems insubstantial to you and limiting your need to be free and explore new possibilities. It is time to turn your head and look in a new direction.

BORN FROM MARCH, 1961 TO FEBRUARY, 1964

Reflect on the time period *May, 1990 to February, 2001.* What major change came about in your life at that time? Depending on when you read this book, the initiators of that change would have been or will be similar to those in the time period *February, 2020 to January, 2023.* What follows is a description of the circumstances that would have surfaced or will surface.

Your life normally has its share of obstacles but now the latest batch of impediments feels enormous. You are doubting your ability to live up to your desired goals and are questioning if your current objectives are practical. Changes are happening such that the role you have worked so hard to achieve is now looking like it has no permanence and is in jeopardy. You are starting to accept the fact that you must move forward, through the upheavals, and emerge on a path leading towards a new goal in life.

Born from March, 1964 to December, 1966

Reflect on the time period *March, 2001 to April, 2003*. Depending on when you read this book, the initiators of that change would have been or will be similar to those in the time period *February, 2023 to April, 2025.* What follows is a description of the circumstances that would have surfaced or will surface.

You are feeling restricted in expressing your point of view. As a result, you are relinquishing your right to individual expression and conforming to a group mandate. This is making you realize just how important your personal freedom is in order for you to live up to your potential and feel fulfilled. You are recognizing just how much you value your personal ingenuity. Deep down you are craving to break loose from the group and dance to your own drummer.

The tribulations that Saturn dishes out must be addressed at one time or another and the sooner the better. Why bother? Saturn guides us and helps clear the way for a treasure of a chance that will enrich our lives. After facing and overcoming these challenges, it is then Jupiter that opens a *door* revealing an opportunity that invites you to pursue your soul's passion.

Jim Morrison of "The Doors" died at the age of 27 in 1971 and was buried in the "Poets Corner" of Père Lachaise Cemetery in Paris. The epitaph on his headstone bears the Greek inscription "KATA TON ΔAIMONA EAYTOY", literally meaning "According to his own daimōn" and usually interpreted as "True to his own spirit". Source: Wikipedia

CHAPTER 4

THE JUPITER OPPORTUNITY KEY

So what is the nature of the opportunity that is revealed to you after you have conscientiously surmounted Saturn's second blitz of trials and tribulations?

We turn to Jupiter's placement in the Zodiac for an answer. Jupiter takes about 12 years to orbit around our Sun and arrive back at the same celestial position it was in when you were born, known as Jupiter transiting your 'natal Jupiter'. When Saturn is making its second go-around at around the age of 60 and is teaching us hard life lessons, you can count on Jupiter making an appearance with its fifth go-around in our lives.

It is Jupiter that possesses the Zodiac's precious key for the door that opens up to reveal a golden opportunity. On Jupiter's fifth encounter with your natal Jupiter, remember that a stern Saturn stands in front of that door. It is not an easy accomplishment for that door to be opened and so the opportunity that is secured is meant to bestow an enduring effect on our lives. In other words, this is a prized opportunity that should be seriously considered.

What follows are particular time periods when this opportunity will come about as well as a description of its unique form. To zero in on a more narrow range of time when Jupiter transits your natal Jupiter position in the sky, you will have to refer to your sidereal astrological birth chart. If this opportunity has already passed by, reflect on how your life changed at this time for the better. This is the manner in which 'Lady Luck' opens the door for success in your life.

BORN FROM JANUARY 1946 TO JANUARY 1947

Depending on when you read this book, a great opportunity came about or will come about in the time period *October 2017 to October 2018.* What follows is a description of the nature of this opportunity:

Your diplomatic approach is highly prized and being honored by others. You are able to recognize just what is necessary to bring about harmony in an otherwise chaotic situation. A close relationship is yielding a breakthrough opportunity and decisive thinking is required to seize the moment.

BORN FROM FEBRUARY 1947 TO FEBRUARY 1948

Depending on when you read this book, a great opportunity came about or will come about in the time period *November 2018 to October 2019.* What follows is a description of the nature of this opportunity:

Bolster your urge to delve into areas that others are too timid to approach. You are a shrewd judge of human character and now is the time to expose the truth and be noble. There will be emotional intensity as you pursue this opportunity but a powerful force is on your side and will boost your energy and confidence.

*"And I think it's gonna be a long long time
Till touch down brings me round again to find
I'm not the man they think I am at home
Oh no, no, no, I'm a rocket man
Rocket man burning out his fuse up here alone"*

Lyrics from "Rocket Man"
by Sir Elton John, 1972

Sir Elton John was born in March, 1947 and received a knighthood from Elizabeth II for "services to music and charitable services" in 1998.

Source: Wikipedia

BORN FROM MARCH 1948 AND FEBRUARY 1949

Depending on when you read this book, a great opportunity came about or will come about in the time period *November 2019 to November 2020.* What follows is a description of the nature of this opportunity:

No word of caution seems to be deterring you from making a leap in faith and charging ahead with a new adventure. Your enthusiasm is overflowing and you are running overtime on high optimism. This opportunity will expand your horizons and deepen your understanding of the meaning of your life.

BORN FROM MARCH 1949 TO MARCH 1950

Depending on when you read this book, a great opportunity came about or will come about in the time period *December 2020 to November 2021.* What follows is a description of the nature of this opportunity:

You are trusted as an authority in your field and you are deeply committed to carrying out your role in this capacity. An opportunity is presenting itself where you have the skill-set and know-how to deliver the required results. Some solitary time contemplating this opportunity will instill in you the confidence you need to accept this offer and afford you the mindset to be indifferent to any opposition.

BORN FROM APRIL 1950 TO MARCH 1951

Depending on when you read this book, a great opportunity came about or will come about in the time period *December 2021 to April 2022.* What follows is a description of the nature of this opportunity:

Regardless of peer pressure and skeptics, your independent spirit is soaring to new heights. An opportunity is in the works for you to freely express your unique ideas and help raise society's intellectual bar. You can be confident that your aspirations can be achieved without having to compromise your individuality.

Born in 1950, Stevie Wonder was named a United Nations Messenger of Peace in 2009.
Source: Wikipedia

"You are the sunshine of my life, yeah

That's why I'll always stay around

You are the apple of my eye

Forever you'll stay in my heart"

Lyrics from "You are the Sunshine of my Life" by Stevie Wonder, 1972

BORN FROM APRIL 1951 TO MARCH 1952

Depending on when you read this book, a great opportunity came about or will come about in the time period *May 2022 to April 2023.* What follows is a description of the nature of this opportunity:

You are experiencing a heightened awareness that almost feels like you are in a lucid dream. An opportunity to open yourself to sacred knowledge and deepen you compassion for all is yours for the taking. Sharing this with others is the ultimate fulfillment.

BORN FROM APRIL 1952 TO MARCH 1953

Depending on when you read this book, a great opportunity came about or will come about in the time period *May 2023 to April 2024.* What follows is a description of the nature of this opportunity:

You are being called on to lead the charge on a pioneering venture. It takes a courageous person for this mission, someone with an intense spirit, determination and abundant energy. You know you fit the bill. This is a unique opportunity meant for your undertaking.

BORN FROM APRIL 1953 TO APRIL 1954

Depending on when you read this book, a great opportunity came about or will come about in the time period *May 2024 to May 2025*. What follows is a description of the nature of this opportunity:

You are rising to the occasion to share with others your interpretation of the wonderful sensations of our world. You are exceedingly skilled at drawing our attention to our human need for pleasure and how important it is to be part of our life. Lady luck is on your side.

BORN FROM MAY 1954 TO SEPTEMBER 1954

Depending on when you read this book, a great opportunity came about or will come about in the time period *June 2025 to May 2026*. What follows is a description of the nature of this opportunity:

An opportunity is arising that calls on your remarkable communication talents. You are admired for your clever mind and ability to adapt to many roles. You have a chance to impress others with your versatility and intellect and leave behind a lasting positive impression.

BORN FROM OCTOBER 1954 TO SEPTEMBER 1955

Depending on when you read this book, a great opportunity came about or will come about in the time period *June 2026 to June 2027.* What follows is a description of the nature of this opportunity:

A heightened sensitivity to the feelings of others is spurring you to step up to the platform and provide an inner understanding of the circumstances. Your genuine support for the well-being of others brings you honor and respect and will be your legacy.

BORN FROM OCTOBER 1955 TO OCTOBER 1956

Depending on when you read this book, a great opportunity came about or will come about in the time period *August 2015 to August 2016.* What follows is a description of the nature of this opportunity:

Your ability to present yourself with great flair and finesse and capture the attention of an audience is extraordinary at this time of your life. Whatever your message is that you want to share with others, this is your golden opportunity to present your mission in a magnanimous manner. Your confidence is high and creativity is abundant. It is the time to win the support of others.

BORN FROM NOVEMBER 1956 TO NOVEMBER 1957

Depending on when you read this book, a great opportunity came about or will come about in the time period *September 2016 to September 2017.* What follows is a description of the nature of this opportunity:

You are discovering ways to improve yourself and this is enhancing your well-being on many levels. Your helpfulness and dedicated service to others is breaking barriers and you are being recognized as a valued associate. An opportunity to advance your stature is at hand.

Michael Jackson, born in 1958, died in 2009.
His 1982 album "Thriller" is the best selling album
of all times.   Source: Wikipedia

BORN FROM DECEMBER 1957 TO DECEMBER 1958

Depending on when you read this book, a great opportunity came about or will come about in the time period *October 2017 to October 2018.* What follows is a description of the nature of this opportunity:

Your diplomatic approach is highly prized and being honored by others. You are able to recognize just what is necessary to bring about harmony in an otherwise chaotic situation. A close relationship is yielding a breakthrough opportunity and decisive thinking is required to seize the moment.

BORN FROM JANUARY 1959 TO JANUARY 1960

Depending on when you read this book, a great opportunity came about or will come about in the time period *November 2018 to October 2019.* What follows is a description of the nature of this opportunity:

Bolster your urge to delve into areas that others are too timid to approach. You are a shrewd judge of human character and now is the time to expose the truth and be noble. There will be emotional intensity as you pursue this opportunity but a powerful force is on your side and will boost your energy and confidence.

BORN FROM FEBRUARY 1960 TO JANUARY 1961

Depending on when you read this book, a great opportunity came about or will come about in the time period *November 2019 to November 2020*. What follows is a description of the nature of this opportunity:

No word of caution seems to be deterring you from making a leap in faith and charging ahead with a new adventure. Your enthusiasm is overflowing and you are running overtime on high optimism. This opportunity will expand your horizons and deepen your understanding of the meaning of your life.

BORN FROM FEBRUARY 1961 AND FEBRUARY 1962

Depending on when you read this book, a great opportunity came about or will come about in the time period *December 2020 to November 2021.* What follows is a description of the nature of this opportunity:

You are trusted as an authority in your field and you are deeply committed to carrying out your role in this capacity. An opportunity is presenting itself where you have the skill-set and know-how to deliver the required results. Some solitary time contemplating this opportunity will instill in you the confidence you need to accept this offer and the mindset to be indifferent to any opposition.

BORN FROM MARCH 1962 TO FEBRUARY 1963

Depending on when you read this book, a great opportunity came about or will come about in the time period *December 2021 to April 2022.* What follows is a description of the nature of this opportunity:

Regardless of peer pressure and skeptics, your independent spirit is soaring to new heights. An opportunity is in the works for you to freely express your unique ideas and help raise society's intellectual bar. You can be confident that your aspirations can be achieved without having to compromise your individuality.

BORN FROM MARCH 1963 TO MARCH 1964

Depending on when you read this book, a great opportunity came about or will come about in the time period *May 2022 to April 2023*. What follows is a description of the nature of this opportunity:

You are experiencing a heightened awareness that almost feels at times like you are in a lucid dream. An opportunity to open yourself to sacred knowledge and deepen your compassion for all is yours for the taking. Sharing your understanding with others is the ultimate fulfillment.

BORN FROM APRIL 1964 TO MARCH 1965

Depending on when you read this book, a great opportunity came about or will come about in the time period *May 2023 to April 2024.* What follows is a description of the nature of this opportunity:

You are being called on to lead the charge on a pioneering venture. It takes a courageous person for this mission, someone with an intense spirit, determination and abundant energy. You know you fit the bill. This is a unique opportunity meant for your undertaking.

CHAPTER 5

WHAT'S IT ALL ABOUT, THIS RETIREMENT?

"What's it all about, Alfie?
Is it just for the moment we live?
What's it all about when you sort it out, Alfie?
Are we meant to take more than we give
Or are we meant to be kind?
And if only fools are kind, Alfie,
Then I guess it's wise to be cruel.
And if life belongs only to the strong, Alfie,
What will you lend on an old golden rule?"

Lyrics from the song "Alfie"
by Burt Bacharach and Hal David, 1966
Written for the Movie "Alfie"
Stars: Michael Caine, Shelley Winters

ZODIAC RETIREMENT MISSIONS

The boomers have been, or will be in the not too distant future, conditioned by Saturn's second assault of disciplining forces. You have dealt, or will be forced to deal with the problems meant for you to face on this planet. By overcoming these challenges, a mature perspective on life develops, along with a greater respect for the need to change one's ways. Now life's obstacles tend not to be as threatening as they used to be; perhaps, you even enjoy the challenges now knowing all tends to work out for the better in the long run.

After Saturn has cleared the path, Jupiter has presented, or will present an opportune time for you to consider a new undertaking, one that will provide you with an exciting fresh start to redirect your life with your unique mission in mind.

Now the question remains, what is your ultimate retirement mission, now that you have "been there and done that"? The Zodiac can provide the answer - it is yours for the taking.

The Sun's Zodiac position reveals your *ultimate mission* on mother Earth. The following description of your Zodiac Retirement Mission is based on your time of birth during the year and it is intentionally not labelled with a Zodiac sign to avoid any biases associated with traditional astrology. *Sidereal astrology* is the celestial placement system being used in this book.

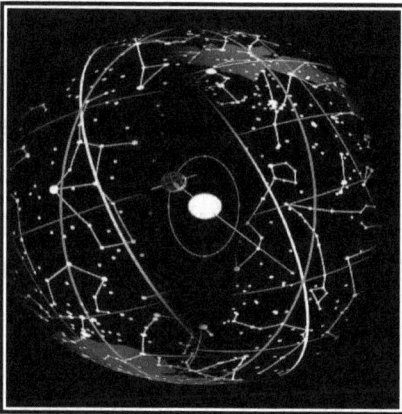

Note: If your birth date falls on the day of transition when the Sun is changing signs at a specific time during that day, you will need a sidereal astrology program to determine your proper Sun sign. For now, you can read the two Missions and judge what one is more akin to you.

BORN FROM APRIL 14 TO MAY 15

Without any hesitation, you are the first person to begin whatever the charge and propel forward, a true pioneer at heart. Scary situations have only spurred you on and you have learned much about courage through some pretty hard life lessons. Through these trials, you have discovered successful ways to overcome your fears and how to avert confrontational situations that end up doing unnecessary harm to yourself.

Take it easy; otherwise, for health reasons you may be forced to withdraw from the competitive game of life for a while. Take time to contemplate what struggles were worth fighting for in your life, such as those that awarded you with personal growth.

Your mission is to voice your opinion to all of those who *need* to hear, as to what challenges, specifically those that require gathering great strength of purpose and courage, are worth striving for and those that are not. Atypically for you, this is a win/win mission.

"Take it easy, take it easy
Don't let the sound of your own wheels drive you crazy
Lighten up while you still can
Don't even try to understand
Just find a place to make your stand, and take it easy"

Lyrics from "Take it Easy" by The Eagles, 1972

No American band sold more records than the Eagles during the 1970s. Source: Wikipedia

BORN FROM MAY 15 TO JUNE 15

With all the hullabaloo in our world, it is difficult to find the time to appreciate the wondrous sounds, smells and feel of nature and human creative expressions. You know only too well the sacrifices asked of you to forfeit these joys over the years. You revere the simplicities of life that require the sound of silence.

You have grown and changed over time with your ability to tolerate and thwart threats to your stability and security. You have comes to terms with what it means for you to be 'safe' in life. Relish the serene beauty that surrounds you and fills you with peaceful feelings as only you can appreciate. As the world swirls around you, you know how to feel at ease.

Your mission is to quietly direct others towards the appreciation of the beauty of our physical world. Beauty is in the eye of the beholder, but there are marvelous physical and sensual creations that should truly never be taken for granted. They feed our souls and make existing on earth simply splendid.

"Now, he walks in quiet solitude
The forests and the streams
Seeking grace in every step he takes
His sight has turned inside
Himself to try and understand
The serenity of a clear blue mountain lake"

Lyrics from "Rocky Mountain High" by John Denver, 1972

John Denver, musician, singer, songwriter, environmentalist, supporter of space exploration, political activist, avid pilot, died in a single-fatality crash of his personal aircraft at the age of 53.

Source: Wikipedia

BORN FROM JUNE 15 TO JULY 17

"Picture yourself in a boat on a river
With tangerine trees and marmalade skies
Somebody calls you, you answer quite slowly
A girl with kaleidoscope eyes
Cellophane flowers of yellow and green
Towering over your head
Look for the girl with the sun in her eyes
And she's gone
Lucy in the sky with diamonds"

Lyrics from "Lucy in the Sky with Diamonds"
by The Beatles, 1967

Your perceptive abilities are truly admirable. Discovering and conveying details that others find obscure is your forte. The computer age has made easy access to information sources and like magic, you are able to instantly respond to your inquisitive mind's queries and satisfy your endless curiosities.

As you know, this information plethora can also lead to a lack of cohesion in your life as well as nervousness and insomnia. You have learned your limits over the years and know that it is necessary to risk boredom by taking a break and turning off the lights in your mind. You also have found out the dire consequences of trying to bamboozle others with your clever talk.

Your mission is to share your best findings, especially what you have discovered in the fields of your endeavors, with all those who are interested. You have the breadth of knowledge to be able to separate the wheat from the chaff and this can prevent researchers from wasting an enormous amount of precious energy.

"I love the colorful clothes she wears
And the way the sunlight plays upon her hair
I hear the sound of a gentle word
On the wind that lifts her perfume through the air
I'm pickin' up good vibrations
She's giving me excitations
Good, good, good, good vibrations"

Lyrics from "Good Vibrations" by The Beach Boys, 1974

The Beach Boys' distinct harmonies gave the boomers a feel for the southern California surfin' lifestyle. "Good Vibrations" is number 6 on Rolling Stone's list of the "500 Greatest Songs of All Time".

BORN FROM JULY 17 TO AUGUST 17

Close your eyes, take in a deep breath and feel the *vibes* - that is how you best interpret life. And you know only too well how your psyche's mood can vacillate with varying intensities like the ocean's tides. You *need to feel* appreciated and loved to make life meaningful for you.

You've learned that emotions are illusory and that trying to rationalize them in words can be a complete waste of time. They are your internal language and over time, after intense interactions with the world, you have grown to accept, trust and love what you have taken to heart. You have developed an appreciation of how fleeting or overwhelming and how powerful or delicate feelings can be.

You understand what vibes are necessary to penetrate and nourish the soul to bring about a sense of fulfillment. Your mission is to engage others in ways that allow them to accept and respect emotions like you do.

BORN FROM AUGUST 17 TO SEPTEMBER 18

Of all the members of the Zodiac family, you know how to appreciate the charismatic expressions of the 'My Generation'. You easily connect with the passion of the performer. The grandness and flow of the creative ego thrusting itself onto the world's stage is the ultimate to you. After all, isn't "All the world's a stage, and all the men and women merely players"?

How very sad you felt when deprived of creative inspiration when you were sidetracked with the mundane obligations demanded of you in life. If only to get back to creating, expressing and simple playfulness; there lies a deep longing. But you have learned to prioritize and attend to life's necessities and appreciate responsibilities.

Here is your mission. Let your energies flow freely and abundantly in your most creative ways. Don't let anything inhibit you from this mission. There are joyful splendors to bubble up from the deep collective consciousness of humanity for you to discover and exuberantly share with others as only you know how to.

"Everybody is a star
I can feel it when you shine on me
I love you for who you are
Not the one you feel you need to be
Ever catch a falling star
Ain't no stopping 'til it's in the ground
Everybody is a star
One big circle going round and round"
Lyrics from "Everybody is a Star" by Sly and the Family Stone, 1970

" In the preface of his 1998 book For the Record: Sly and the Family Stone: An Oral History, Joel Selvin sums up the importance of Sly and the Family Stone's influence on African American music by stating "there are two types of black music: black music before Sly Stone, and black music after Sly Stone". The band was inducted into the Rock and Roll Hall of Fame in 1993."

Quote from: Wikipedia

"When you're weary, feeling small,
When tears are in your eyes, I will dry them all;
I'm on your side. When times get rough
And friends just can't be found,
Like a bridge over troubled water
I will lay me down.
Like a bridge over troubled water
I will lay me down."

Lyrics from "Bridge over Troubled Water"
by Simon and Garfunkel, 1970. This song was the
duo's biggest hit single.   Source: Wikipedia

BORN FROM SEPTEMBER 18 TO OCTOBER 18

Your cool logic, deep sense of responsibility and strong ethics bestow the perfect 'bridge over troubled water' to help heal, protect and maintain our fragile human dignity.

You have learned not to judge yourself too harshly and you have come to a deep understanding that you are your own best friend. You know that you must forgive yourself for any indiscretions. You recognize that trivial details that tend to overwhelm have to be disregarded in order for you to maintain your vigor.

The world has to progress in an honorable and transparent manner to foster the value of equity. We all need to include your qualities of pureness, integrity and your virtue of being of useful service to others in our lives. Don't listen to anyone who tells you otherwise. Your mission is to carry out your praiseworthy principles in the way that *you* find most effective. No one else can foster divine perfection like you can.

A major attraction at the "Woodstock" festival in 1969, Janice Joplin is known as "The Queen of Psychedelic Soul". Janice died in 1970 at the age of 27. Source: Wikipedia

"Don't you know, honey,
Ain't nobody ever gonna love you
The way I try to do
Who'll take all your pain
Honey, your heartache, too
And if you need me, you know
That I'll always be around if you ever want me
Come on and cry, cry baby, cry baby, cry baby"

Lyrics from "Cry Baby" by Janice Joplin

BORN FROM OCTOBER 18 TO NOVEMBER 17

Life is a balancing act between joy and sorrow, patience and edginess, practicalities and ideals and you know that being at the center evokes peace. If a life challenge is akin to creating a painting, you know precisely how to distribute splashes of color and light around the 'center of attention' of the composition. You are a born diplomat.

Over the years you have struggled with achieving this center position as it never comes easily. It has often meant compromises and sometimes sacrificing your heart's wishes for the sake of your partner's. Your inner wisdom knows that there really are no true winners/losers in life, but that everyone wins when there's harmony.

Your mission is to use your expertise as a peace maker to assist others to be in accord without having to sacrifice their natural genuineness. Individuality is a sacred right and the world is a better place having your wisdom to help us harmonize our differences.

BORN FROM NOVEMBER 17 TO DECEMBER 16

Nothing escapes your gaze and there really isn't anything that you can't look at straight in the eye. Many would shy away from tense situations, but you actually thrive on them. And you will passionately strip away the superficial layers to expose the underlying truth, as only you can.

Such an acute, intuitive awareness of phoniness has led you to be overly suspicious of others and adopt a tendency to doubt their sincerity. Your shrewd, dissecting mind thrives on digging up the reasons why you shouldn't trust them.

"Why you try to put up a front for me

I'm a spy but on your side you see

Slip on, into any disguise

I'll still know you

Look into my Private Eyes

Private Eyes

They're watching you

They see your every move"

Lyrics from "Private Eyes" by Daryl Hall and John Oates, 1981

Life experiences have taught you the hard way to give some slack to people's behaviors after losing friends that you mercilessly investigated.
You have realized that some superficialities are not really intended to be taken seriously, and that some people you thought were not trustworthy were actually sincere allies. Your evolved motto is 'not guilty until proven guilty'.

Your mission: We need your astute radar for discerning fact from fiction as our world has a crucial need for honesty. Deceptive tactics to instill fear in the hearts of many permeate our society. You know only too well from experience how overwhelming emotions and negative thoughts can eat away at the spirit. The truth is precious and yours to disclose for our benefit.

"Billboard" magazine has named Hall and Oates the most successful duo of the rock era. They were inducted into the Rock and Roll Hall of Fame in 2014.

Source: Wikipedia

BORN FROM DECEMBER 16 TO JANUARY 14

Life to you is an adventure, both physically and mentally. You thrive on new encounters in many forms - people, places, studies. You want to continually expand your awareness and comprehend the totality of life. Instinctively, in your quest, you know how to draw from the deep, sacred lake of inspirational energy.

You sense you can realize your intended full potential if you can find the meaning of life that rings true to your heart. Crushing lessons have taught you that your enthusiasm can be seriously taken advantage of by others who recognize your innocent vulnerability. Your personal freedom and respect are values that you have learned to cherish. You have become very frank in defending these values.

The world needs someone with high ideals and spirit to venture into the unknown for the benefit of expanding our collective awareness. For it is you who can make what seemed unimaginable a conscious realization. We call on you to take on this noble and daring mission.

"We are the world
We are the children
We are the ones who make a brighter day
So let's start giving
There is a choice we're making
We're saving our own lives
It's true we'll make a better day, just you and
me"
Lyrics from "We are the World"

USA for Africa (United Support of Artists for Africa) was the name under which 44 predominantly U.S. artists, led by Michael Jackson and Lionel Richie, recorded the hit single "We Are the World" in 1985.
Source: Wikipedia

BORN FROM JANUARY 14 TO FEBRUARY 13

Steadfast, determined, through thick or thin, you are the one who gets the job done. It is you that is the expert in bringing together inner motives with outward expressions. Your ambitions are realized through smart and diligent work.

You have learned not to play to the crowd. Setbacks in your life have arisen whenever you have thoughtlessly compromised your integrity and succumbed to the hook of social affirmation. Having your own self-respect is what matters. Success comes by keeping a solitary, logical mind that seeks approval from only yourself. This has brought you admiration and has set you apart from the crowd.

Your retirement mission is now to turn your eyes to the world with your mature point of view on global power. We need your disciplined way of thinking to help us harness mankind's highest form of expression with our thoughts firmly rooted in mother Earth's nourishing ground.

In 2012, The Rolling Stones celebrated their 50th anniversary as a band. "Rolling Stone" magazine ranked them fourth on the "100 Greatest Artists of All Time" list, and their estimated album sales are above 250 million.

Source: Wikipedia

"You can't always get what you want
You can't always get what you want
You can't always get what you want
But if you try sometimes you just might find
You just might find
You get what you need"
Lyrics from "You Can't Always Get What You Want" by The Rolling Stones, 1969

Robert Plant was the lead vocalist of the band "Led Zeppelin". In 2011, Rolling Stone magazine ranked Plant as the great of all lead singers. Source: Wikipedia

"And as we wind on down the road
Our shadows taller than our soul
There walks a lady we all know
Who shines white light and wants to show
How everything still turns to gold

And if you listen very hard
The tune will come to you at last
When all are one and one is all, yeah
To be a rock and not to roll

And she's buying a stairway to heaven"
Lyrics from "Stairway to Heaven" by Led Zeppelin, 1971

BORN FROM FEBRUARY 13 TO MARCH 15

Genius, yes, you have the capability to think like no one else. You do not compromise as that would be a betrayal to your sense of individuality and personal freedom. You make your choices based on what you believe to be true, regardless of what anyone else thinks. You thrive on bringing about innovative change with the honest intent of improving society's welfare. You are not after personal glory.

Your independent and stubborn ways have given you a reputation of being eccentric, yet you still resist conforming as you know your heart is in the right place. On the other hand, you have gained a greater respect for conventionality and it is not as much of an adversary as it was for you in your younger years.

Your mission is to challenge the status quo in ways that only you know stand a chance of taking hold in our society. There are many important global issues that we have to address as we evolve into a world of oneness and we need your genius to reveal solutions.

BORN FROM MARCH 15 TO APRIL 14

They may say you are a 'dreamer', but you are not the only one, thank goodness. For you know how to connect us to the mystic ocean of the *collective consciousness*, our essential source of universal wisdom. That connection tends to take you away from the realities of everyday life, afloat in your awareness of the world from a heavenly perspective.

Alas, the necessary exertion to sustain relationships and carry out day-to-day responsibilities are constantly bringing you back down to earth. Life has brought its share of frustrations knowing that others do not place the same value as you do on *unseen* concepts. Those that say "To see is to believe" you believe are naïve. Yet, you are a peace-loving, compassionate individual who has little desire for confrontation and typically lets it be.

You have the ultimate of missions: the world is crying out for the wisdom of how we can live as *'one'*. Show us the way, oh wise one connected with the ocean of the collective consciousness.

"Imagine there's no heaven
It's easy if you try
No hell below us
Above us only sky
Imagine all the people living
for today
......
You may say
I'm a dreamer, but I'm not
the only one
I hope someday you'll join us
And the world will live as
one."
Lyrics from "Imagine" by
John Lennon, 1971

John Lennon was inducted into the Rock and Roll Hall of Fame twice; once as a member of the Beatles in 1988 and again as a solo artist in 1994. Rolling Stone magazine ranked him as the 5th greatest singer of all time.

Source: Wikipedia

FINAL WORDS FOR MY GENERATION

You have reaped life experiences that have added to your own innate pool of wisdom. It is now the time to add this knowledge to the ocean of our collective human wisdom. By doing so, you will fulfill your potential as a unique soul.

Happy retirement days to all. ☮

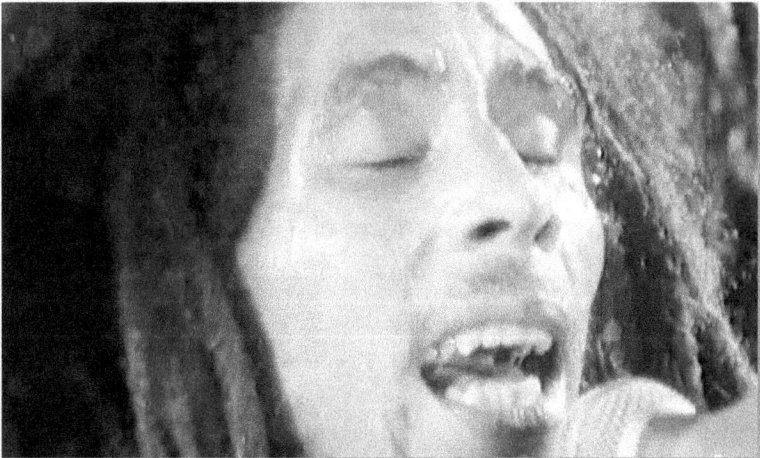

Bob Marley, April 1977
One Love Peace Concert
Courtesy "Heartland Reggae"

"Money Secrets of the Zodiac" delves into the depths of the twelve Zodiac archetypes and exposes their true money-motivating desires. Such insights can empower you by bringing to light why you and others approach and handle money the way you do. When it comes to money issues in a relationship between two individuals, traits that work well together and those that clash are revealed. This book can sharpen your acumen about the money mindset of the individual you are planning to partner with which is crucial to know if you are going to be making major financial decisions together. As a reference guide, you can quickly zero-in on details concerning a specific personality or relationship. You will find yourself referring to this book's pages many times as your life unfolds and challenging money issues arise.

A must read for anyone interested in how money affects lives and relationships.

Stephanie Venn, B Sc. MBA CFP, has over 20 years experience in sharing personal financial advice.

Priceless information for financial advisors

Money Secrets of the ZODIAC

by Stephanie Venn

www.ingramcontent.com/pod-product-compliance
Lightning Source LLC
Chambersburg PA
CBHW031729210326
41520CB00042B/1503